MARS

by L. L. Owens

The Child's World®

Published by The Child's World®
1980 Lookout Drive • Mankato, MN 56003-1705
800-599-READ • www.childsworld.com

ACKNOWLEDGMENTS
The Child's World®: Mary Berendes, Publishing Director
The Design Lab: Design and production
Red Line Editorial: Editorial direction

PHOTO CREDITS
NASA/Goddard Space Flight Center Scientific Visualization Studio/courtesy of
nasaimages.org, cover, 1, 32; NASA/courtesy of nasaimages.org, cover, 1, 3, 4, 6,
11, 14, 16, 19, 20, 24, 26, 31; NASA/NSSDC/Catalog of Spaceborne Imaging,
5, 25; NASA/courtesy of nasaimages.org/The Design Lab, 6, 7; NASA/Goddard
Space Flight Center Scientific Visualization Studio/courtesy of nasaimages.org/The
Design Lab, 9; NASA/JPL-Caltech/University of Arizona/courtesy of nasaimages.
org, 13, 21; Mikhail Khromov/iStockphoto, 15; NASA/JPL-Caltech/courtesy of
nasaimages.org, 17; NASA/JPL/University of Arizona/courtesy of nasaimages.org,
23; NASA/JPL/MSSS/courtesy of nasaimages.org, 27; Will Kincaid/AP Images, 29

LIBRARY OF CONGRESS CATALOGING-IN-PUBLICATION DATA
Owens, L. L.
 Mars / by L.L. Owens.
   p. cm.
 Includes bibliographical references and index.
 ISBN 978-1-60954-383-9 (library bound : alk. paper)
 1. Mars (Planet)—Juvenile literature. I. Title.
 QB641.O94 2011
 523.43—dc22
                          2010039960

Printed in the United States of America
Mankato, MN
December, 2010
PA02072

ON THE COVER
Artists and scientists created this image of Mars showing the planet's true colors.

Table of Contents

Mars and the Solar System, 4

Humans and Mars, 14

A Hard, Rocky Planet, 20

Weather on Mars, 26

Glossary, 30

Further Information, 31

Index, 32

Mars and the Solar System

Try looking near the moon after sunset. Do you see what looks like a bright orange star? That's Mars! Mars is one of our space neighbors in the **solar system**. At the center of our solar system is the sun. Planets go around, or **orbit**, the sun.

Fun Fact

Mars is known as the Red Planet. From space it looks like a glowing orange-red ball.

The *Viking* spacecraft took images of the planet Mars in 1980.

SUN

Mercury

Venus

Earth

Mars

Ceres

Jupiter

Fun Facts

PLANET NUMBER: Mars is the fourth planet from the sun.

DISTANCE FROM SUN: 142 million miles (229 million km)

SIZE: Mars is about 13,263 miles (21,345 km) around the middle. To run that far would be like running the bases on a baseball field almost 200,000 times!

OUR SOLAR SYSTEM: Our solar system has eight planets and five **dwarf planets**. Pluto used to be called a planet. But in 2006, scientists decided to call it a dwarf planet instead. Scientists hope to discover even more dwarf planets in our solar system!

Saturn

Uranus

Neptune

Pluto

Haumea

Makemake

Eris

Planet

Dwarf Planet

While orbiting the sun, a planet spins like a top. Each planet spins, or rotates, on its **axis**. An axis is an imaginary line that runs through the planet from top to bottom. One rotation equals one day. Think of one day on a planet as the time from one sunrise to the next sunrise.

Mars rotates on its axis once every 24 hours and 40 minutes. That's about the same length as one Earth day.

An axis runs through the center of a planet. The planet spins on the axis.

A year is the time it takes for a planet to travel around the sun once. A year on Earth is about 365 days. But Mars travels very slowly. It takes Mars 687 days to go around the sun once. That makes a year on Mars almost twice as long as a year on Earth.

Images of Mars (right) and Earth are placed next to each other to show how much bigger Earth is than Mars.

While Mars orbits the sun, two small moons orbit Mars—Phobos (FOE-bos) and Deimos (DYE-mos). The moons are dark gray and made of ice and rock.

Phobos is covered with 3 feet (.9 m) of dust. It orbits very close to Mars. Scientists expect it will crash into Mars someday. Deimos is the smallest known moon in the solar system. Both moons have deep **craters**.

These two views of Deimos show some of the moon's craters.

Humans and Mars

Mars has fascinated humans for thousands of years. It is one of the planets you can see from Earth without a **telescope**.

Romans studied the planet more than 2,000 years ago. Its red color reminded them of blood. They named it Mars after their fierce god of war.

Fun Fact

Mars's surface is covered in a red mineral called iron. This is what gives Mars its rusty color.

This statue of Mars, the Roman god of war, is in Russia.

No one has ever walked on Mars, but scientists think it might be possible someday. Scientists have sent spacecraft to land on the planet. The spacecraft gather rocks from the surface. In 2010, a NASA spacecraft took exciting new pictures of Mars. It gave us a very detailed map of the planet.

Fun Fact

NASA stands for the National Aeronautics and Space Administration. It is a US agency that studies space and the planets.

A NASA rover that landed on Mars took this picture on the planet's surface in 2009.

All life as we know it needs water. Some scientists believe that liquid water once existed on Mars. This water might have carved out the empty valleys that exist on the planet today.

Ice exists in some of Mars's coldest places. Some scientists think tiny life forms might live on Mars today. This would make Mars the second planet in our solar system with life on it!

This spacecraft was sent to Mars to look for water.

A Hard, Rocky Planet

Scientists know that Mars has mountains, canyons, and volcanoes, like Earth. Mars is a **terrestrial** planet. Other planets are made of **gas** with no hard surface.

Fun Fact

There are two types of planets.

TERRESTRIAL PLANETS (mostly rock) are close to the sun. They are: Mercury, Venus, Earth, and Mars.

GAS GIANTS (mostly gas and liquid) are farther from the sun. They are: Jupiter, Saturn, Uranus, and Neptune.

Wind and ice have shaped
the landforms on Mars's
surface.

21

Millions of years ago, **meteorites** crashed into Mars. They created many deep craters. If oceans and rivers existed, they dried up. This left flat, smooth plains and deep canyons.

These two craters on Mars are
each about half a mile
(.8 km) across.

Mars has the deepest canyons and highest mountains of any planet in our solar system. Valles Marineris (VAL-uhs mar-uh-NAIR-is) is called the Grand Canyon of Mars. Imagine standing on a stack of 22 Empire State Buildings and looking down. The ground would be 6 miles (9.7 km) away—as deep as parts of Valles Marineris!

Fun Fact

Olympus Mons is the tallest volcano on Mars—and in the entire solar system. Its base is about as big as Arizona. Scientists have never seen it erupt.

Pictures taken by spacecraft were pieced together to show part of Valles Marineris.

25

Weather on Mars

A planet's **atmosphere** is the layer of gas around it. Earth's atmosphere is the air that we breathe. Mars's atmosphere is very thin. There's just enough of it to create dust clouds and high winds on the surface below. Dust storms are common on Mars.

Fun Fact

In the late 1800s, scientists saw streaks on Mars that they couldn't explain. Some people feared aliens they called Martians had made them. But the streaks were caused by dust storms.

Spacecraft take pictures to
track weather on Mars.

Mars is colder than Earth. The average temperature is −80°F (−60°C). That feels like the coldest-ever day in Alaska.

But with special equipment, humans could walk on the surface of Mars. Maybe you'll be the first!

A college student tests a possible Mars space suit in a rocky area of North Dakota.

29

GLOSSARY

atmosphere (AT-muhss-fihr): An atmosphere is the mixture of gases around a planet or a star. Mars has a thin atmosphere.

axis (AK-siss): An axis is an imaginary line that runs through the center of a planet or a moon. Mars rotates on its axis.

craters (KRAY-turz): Craters are large areas on the surface of a moon or a planet that dip down, like bowls. Mars has many craters on its surface.

dwarf planets (DWORF PLAN-itz): Dwarf planets are round bodies in space that orbit the sun, are not moons, and are not large enough to clear away their paths around the sun. Dwarf planets often have similar objects that orbit near them.

gas (GASS): A gas is a substance that moves around freely and can spread out. Some planets are made mostly of gas.

meteorites (MEE-tee-ur-ryts): Meteorites are small rocks that travel through a planet's atmosphere and crash onto the surface. Meteorites crashed onto Mars's surface and created craters.

mineral (MIN-ur-uhl): A mineral is a natural substance that is not a plant or an animal. The surface of Mars is covered in a mineral called iron.

orbit (OR-bit): To orbit is to travel around another body in space, often in an oval path. Planets orbit the sun.

solar system (SOH-lur SISS-tum): Our solar system is made up of the sun, eight planets and their moons, and smaller bodies that orbit the sun. Mars is the fourth planet from the sun in our solar system.

telescope (TEL-uh-skope): A telescope is a tool that makes faraway objects appear closer. Mars is one planet we can see from Earth without a telescope.

terrestrial (tuh-RESS-tree-uhl): Terrestrial describes planets that have firm land, like Earth. Mars is a terrestrial planet.

FURTHER INFORMATION

BOOKS

O'Brien, Patrick. *You Are the First Kid on Mars*. New York: G. P. Putnam's Sons, 2009.

Trammel, Howard K. *The Solar System*. New York: Children's Press, 2010.

Zobel, Derek. *Mars*. Minnetonka, MN: Bellwether Media, 2010.

WEB SITES

Visit our Web site for links about Mars: **childsworld.com/links**

Note to Parents, Teachers, and Librarians: We routinely verify our Web links to make sure they are safe and active sites. So encourage your readers to check them out!

INDEX

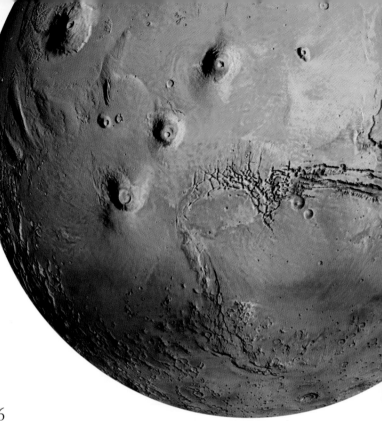

atmosphere, 26

Deimos, 12
distance from sun, 6

length of day, 8
length of year, 10

name, 14
NASA, 16

Olympus Mons, 24

Phobos, 12

size, 6
studying the planet, 14, 16, 18, 24, 26
sun, 4, 6, 8, 10, 12
surface, 14, 16, 18, 20, 22, 24, 26, 28

temperature, 28

Valles Marineris, 24

water, 18, 22

ABOUT THE AUTHOR

L. L. Owens has been writing books for children since 1998. She writes both fiction and nonfiction and especially loves helping kids explore the world around them.